BLOOD RAW: AN ORAL HISTORY OF ADDICTION, RECOVERY & TRIUMPH

By Alphonsa Davis

Copyright © 2014

All rights reserved

ISBN:1505411785

AL'S DEDICATION

This book is dedicated to all my family members who stuck with me through the good times and the bad times. We are still friends, and our hearts are still filled with love. I thank all of you for your heartfelt sacrifices.

CONTENTS

	Introduction	5
1	Moonshiners & Madness: The Beginning	8
2	Picking Cherries	15
3	Mexican Mud & Finding God	34
4	Recovery Years	42

Al's Introduction

We have been told so many different stories about how people become addicted, and also about what is involved concerning Heroin addiction, that I thought that I might like to add my insight on this controversial matter. My name is Alphonsa Davis, and I was a serious Heroin addict for upwards of twenty-eight years. I would like to share with you the events and circumstances that shaped my drug-addicted lifestyle, and also the many happenstances that caused me to suffer this malady for so many, many, years. This is a journey that took me from the east coast to the west coast, from Florida to New York City, from Miami Beach and the Atlantic to Los Angeles and the Pacific, from Santa Monica to Puget Sound in Seattle, Washington, and the Space Needle; the largest spike in North America. I was once working at the Seattle Convention Center for a party sponsored by Microsoft's then Chairman, Bill Gates. We had a bathroom break and upon entering the bathroom, I heard two other cooks who were working with me discussing this guy who had these tremendous amounts of spike marks on his arm. They were laughing about how this guy must have come to

Seattle because he was trying to find the largest spike to shoot his Heroin with, which would be Seattle's Space Needle. I didn't pay it any attention until it dawned on me that they were talking about me.

Inadvertently, while we were working, I had rolled up the sleeves of my shirt and all the tracks on my arm had been exposed, and the tracks were still raw. I was so embarrassed, but that still didn't stop me from shooting my dope. At that time, a train wreck couldn't have prevented me from getting high.

My purpose for discussing these matters is to inform anyone who is getting high of off Heroin, Methadone, Morphine, Lora tabs, Percocet, Oxycodone, OxyContin, Dilaudid, Roxy's and a host of other opioids that almost all of my dope shooting friends and partners are no longer present in the land of the living. They haven't been in the land of the living for quite some time now. Why am I still here? If I knew the answer to that question I would be able to answer the "Sixty-four Thousand Dollar Question", and probably be able to write a book about it. If you shoot these products, you are playing Russian roulette with your life. I can't count the times that I have overdosed on Heroin, and have awakened in a daze, sometimes having been unconscious for many hours. Once I did too big a shot and was in a place full of thieves and vultures that would strip me bare if I was to pass out. So I staggered down the stairs, and just made it to my vehicle, and started up the car and proceeded to pass out. This was at about 9:00 in the morning. When I came up out of my nod, it was 5:00 that evening and that old Wildcat Buick was still humming. Luckily for me, I had the windows down, and the killers and thieves hadn't noticed me. The dope that morning was a fresh batch, and the dealers were trying to O.D. some of their clients to get the word out about how potent their product was. I almost became one of their selling points. Nobody would have cared but my folks, nobody in the dope world, would have given a shit.

I have been clean for 13 to 14 years now. I would never have believed that there would come a time when I was not shooting Heroin. I have gone to great lengths to shoot my dope, I have committed thousands and thousands of crimes to obtain my fix, and I have spent vast sums of money over the years to ingest the China Whites, The Mexican-Mud, The Boy, Skag, Junk, Dilaudid, Oxy, Roxie, Liquid Methadone, and all the other opioids. At the end of the day, they are still here, and they are still just as dangerous as ever, and they are still killing people. Don't you become one of the statistics.

Moonshiners and Madness:
The Beginning

All stories must begin somewhere so I will have my story begin at the age of nine, although it began much earlier than that. Ours was a close-knit family that always interacted with the family unit as one. We were poor but we never went hungry, or never had our lights turned off for non-payment, nor were we ever evicted from anywhere. I guess you have to have something to be thankful for so those facts will have to suffice.

We were a family of alcoholics, beginning with my maternal grandfather. He singled-handily built his own home from scratch on land that he had subscripted in 1919. He staked out four parcels of land that stayed in the family until the Subprime Loan debacle of 2008. A lot of my family got hurt with that. Anyway, not only was he a great builder, but he was also a moonshiner and an alcoholic. I can't ever remember him having worked for anyone other than himself. He was a butcher, and also a great one with barbecuing exotic meats. In those days, there was a great demand for individuals who could cure and prepare wild game, and that is where my grandfather came in.

There was also an alcoholic substance called, "Home-brew," which only my grandfather could make. Evidently, he also made a pretty penny for being one of the only people who could make this intoxicating drink. I can still remember hearing stories about my grandfather being put in jail in those long-ago, older days of our hometown when the city jail could only hold four people, and my grandfather would be one of those. He never stayed any longer than he could sleep one of his drunks off. He was a remarkable man to the white folks in those long-ago days of "Jim Crow". I was his favorite grandson and he nick-named me "Sonny-boy".

My aunt was a notorious bootlegger. She had lots of inherited land, and also a cluster of rooming houses. Needless to say, all of the adults in our semi-large family drank because of the abundance of sealed liquor, beer, and "Home-brew," that was floating around the premises. The only adult in our sphere that I never saw take a single drink was my father, although he stood little chance of changing the family dynamics because he was outnumbered by the sheer amount of family members that were semi-involved in those bootlegging activities. Most of us resided in wooden houses, and I can still remember having false bottoms cut into the floors to hide the liquor from view. Afterward, you would just have to place a rug on the floor, and no one would ever know that under the floorboards were hiding places for the liquor and other products.

I was born with asthma, and the earliest known treatment of any consequences for asthma was a pill called "Primatene." It caused the airways to open up so that the asthmatic could get oxygen into his or her lungs. It was quite effective, but it also was awfully strong. It was loaded with epinephrine and adrenaline, but it did the job. I would be running around like a madman, and bouncing off the walls with uncapped energy. I didn't know what was going on, I was only six years of age, and was already a speed junkie. I was only supposed to take a half of a pill, but when I came to realize that if I took a whole pill, I could outrun and outfight everybody. Even though I was a runt for my age, picking a fight with me and expecting to win that fight, with me at that speed; all bets were off. People would notice us kids playing and would ask the question, "what is up with that kid; he is non-stop action like he is on something"? And I was. If my mother thought anything she never let on, they were just glad that I had found something that could keep me alive, because many, many, times I had quit breathing because I couldn't find one more breath. To still be here today, is a miracle in itself.

A few of my friends and I were about nine or ten years of age when we thought that we would like to have us smoke like our parents always did when they wanted to relax. So we stole some cigarettes out of my mother's pack, and we all lit up. That was the most god-awful taste that I had ever encountered, and everybody was coughing, so we hurried up and threw those terrible things away. A few months later, one of our friends chanced upon a little cigar called "Swisher Sweets," that was almost like smoking candy, and pretty soon all of the young boys were smoking those. I would end up smoking cigarettes for the next thirty years.

We lived in a small agricultural town where all the young boys would go to work on the weekends picking fruit, or "harvesting oranges" as it was actually called. It was back-breaking work, and you had to have a strong constitution to be any good at it. It was extremely physically-demanding, back-breaking work. You also had to be ambidextrous, and extremely fast with your hands. I was tiny, but I was also extremely fast and excelled at picking oranges. The ladders were so heavy that I could not lift them, so I had to role my ladder around the trees. I would make nice sums of money on those weekends, and on those weekend nights, me and my friends would go out bar-hopping, looking for girls, and getting drunk. I was thirteen years of age.

I had started drinking when one of our relatives came down to Florida from Alabama and had made us some homemade wine. I did not have any knowledge of family dynamics, and coming from a family with a legion of alcoholics; I was already pre-disposed to alcoholism. What really got me started drinking so young was one Saturday evening at the corner store that also doubled as a bar, a bunch of Jamaican fruit-pickers was having a beer drinking party, and the tables were loaded with these beers. Surely they would not miss one of those beers if I took one, so I did. So I went outside drank the beer, and started to feel pretty good, so I went back inside and took another one. By the time I got home, I was as drunk as "Cooter Brown", and Cooter Brown was a legendary alcoholic. I went to bed so nobody would notice how drunk I was, I was probably about twelve years old then, going on thirteen.

Every weekend I would go to work, buy an outfit, and a hat, and get intoxicated on Saturday night, throw up in my new hat, and get carried home on the shoulders of my lifetime friend "Katman". He was also an alcoholic, but he could outdrink me. I don't remember how many hats I threw away, but it was quite a few. My family would try to dissuade me from getting drunk in the streets, and having to be brought home every weekend, but how can a bunch of drunks question you about getting drunk, when every weekend they too would get drunk? The whole neighborhood and most of the black community was just "living for the weekend", so they too could party and get drunk.

How I finished high-school at 16 years of age is a wonder to me inasmuch as I very seldom studied and was always running the streets and partying with some of my bad friends. I had this one friend who was an armed robber. He wouldn't take me out on his "jobs" because he didn't want to incur the wrath of my mother and my father. He said that I had a future because I once had been an exceptionally bright lad, long before the alcohol, and the other distractions had taken their effects on me. Yet and still, he didn't want to be blamed for anything bad happening to me while on one of his capers. Luckily for me that he wouldn't take me out with him, because he eventually ended up with a 115-year sentence for armed robbing a store, and kidnapping the female store clerk at gunpoint, and using her as a hostage to walk through a cluster of police who had trapped him inside the store. He escaped that trap, only he went home, and they captured him at his girlfriend's house. He was a known armed robber; I could never figure out why he would go back home to his own neighborhood. He eventually got out of prison and raised 8 head of children before he died. He never got into any kind of trouble again.

We had never seen any hard drugs in my little country town, but after I had joined the Air Force at 18, I was shocked to see the amount of hard drugs that were being ingested by the troops.

Picking Cherries

I finished high school at sixteen years of age going on 17. In those days you could not get a job if you weren't 18 years of age, so all that was left for me to do was to hang out with the unsavory elements of the town that didn't have a job, nor was looking for a job, and didn't want to have a job. I didn't go to college because my drinking, and chasing girls, and being a malcontent, had caused my grades to drop, and a scholarship was out of the question. Therefore, I was stuck in a little hole, without a window to see through, as far as my educational choices were concerned. I suppose I could have gone and picked some oranges, but I refused to finish high school just to go and pick oranges; something any vagrant could do.

There was a criminal element in our little town that was located outside of the city limits, and they operated a house of prostitution, a gambling den, an open bar, and on the weekends they had live bands, and Las Vegas type shows which they named "Las

Vegas Reviews". All of these activities were illegal, but since the county sheriff was a party to this; the police just turned their heads, and allowed these activities to proceed.

There would be a shooting and or a killing almost every weekend. This is where I encountered my first taste of the other side of the law. This is where we did the majority of our drinking and hell raising. There was this one prostitute who had a penchant for young boys, and she took a shining to me for some reason. She was breathtaking. She was 24 years of age, and I was just sixteen. She would keep me in beer and wine, and a few dollars, although I drew the line on having her give me her prostitution money, although she tried. I told her my daddy was a real man, and his son didn't need anybody to give him any money because real men make their own money.

The year that I finished High School, a bunch of us decided to go to Michigan to pick cherries, just for the summer. We were going with this man that knew all of our families, so he could be trusted to look after us properly. Some of the young boys were still in high school. My prostitute friend asked me where I was going, and I told her that I was going to Michigan with my friends to pick cherries and make me some pocket money. We left for Michigan on this dirty, rusty, tramp bus, but for us it was an adventure, and we thought that we would have much fun. I think I might have just turned seventeen. Anyway, we got to Perry, Florida, which is about two or three hundred miles from our hometown. We looked out of the windows of the bus, and much to our surprise, a car was following us. We were stopped at a store to get some gas, and to pick up some snacks, when onto the bus strode this real beautiful, fine, red-boned, voluptuous female, wearing a large blonde wig, and skintight clothing, revealing every wonderful curve that she had. She came right to my seat, and sat down beside me on those dusty seats and said to me," You know you can't leave me, wherever you are going, I'm going also", and she did. I was sort of embarrassed, and also kind of proud to have someone of her stature to single me out for attention. I was also embarrassed because all of my friends knew that she was a whore from out of the whorehouse. Yet and still, I was proud because I was the only one having someone so fine following him.

We got to Michigan, and we stayed in one camp, but because space was limited, she had to stay on another migrant camp. On the weekends, we would take the bus and go around to the other camps in the area, drinking and partying. She tried to sell herself to get me some money so I wouldn't have to pick cherries, but I refused to allow it. This was my adventure, and I didn't want it to be the start of a Pimping career. Everybody called me crazy because there were only two loose women in the whole area, and I had one of them, and my brother had the other one. After I wouldn't let her whore for me, she got mad at me; disgusted would be a better word for it; and she eventually moved on. I don't know why I had such pride, I would sometimes be dead broke, and would still be talking smack. The cherry picking was a disaster, but I made me some money picking apples and went back home.

On the way back home, on the Greyhound bus, we had a layover in Baltimore, Maryland. I decided to go and have a drink at this bar when I was approached by this stranger. He said to me that he was looking for the Pea-Green Hotel, and if I helped him find this hotel, he would pay me handsomely, because "he couldn't read and wrote em so well." He then proceeded to pull out this wad of money as if to pay me if I would help him. I suppose that he singled me out because I looked like a country bumpkin, and he just knew that I was a greenhorn. I must have looked like money also because I did have a fair amount of apple-picking money on me. It was lucky for me that I had been in that whorehouse in my hometown because I noticed the undershirt that the stranger was wearing was made of silk. There was this pimp named David who only wore silk underwear, and why would this supposedly, illiterate, country man be wearing silk underwear? Only true pimps and players wore silk underwear in those days because those items were expensive, and the common man could not afford them. That knowledge saved me a lot of pain, my apple-picking money, and possibly my life. These were con-men trying to lure me off, and relieve me of my money, and maybe also my life. At that knowledge, I bristled with anger, and said to him and his other partner waiting in the wings, "you all are lucky I don't have my pistol with me because I would sure take you to the Pea-green hotel and bury yawls asses." Then they said a strange thing to me. They said, "Young blood you woke up on time, you will surely be a great player in your time. Take that mark ass shirt off, and don't wear it ever again. It makes you look like a sucker". Then they had them a quick laugh and walked off. For the remainder of the bus ride home, I thought about how my circumstances had sort of prepared me not to be a victim of a lot of things.

I got back home, and the same-old-same-old situation was still staring me in the face; what to do with myself. It was during this time that I became indoctrinated into some of the things of the underworld. There were surely plenty of teachers around. I only had this one teacher, who was an older fellow, and he took me under his wings and showed me how to stay out of the way of the card and dice tricks that the slicksters at the whorehouse were using to break all the marks.

Eventually, the prostitutes moved on, and I was back to square one, with nothing to do until I saw one of my ex-classmates, walking down the street, decked out in this blue uniform that said "The United States Air Force." Although I was not supposed to even try that because of my medical condition, I was determined to try. I had to do something; I was drowning in mediocrity. I was seventeen when I went to the recruitment office and applied for the service. I was eventually accepted and went on to basic training. How I survived that grueling adventure is a testament to the power of a real God.

I went on to Tech School, and that is when I ran into that demon called 'drugs.' With all that gambling, and prostitution, and drinking that I had been exposed too, I still had never had an encounter with any illicit drugs. One night in Tech School some guys from Texas said, "hey Florida, come over here." They said, "Here try this; this will put some hair on your chest." That was my very first encounter with marijuana.

We started smoking weed every weekend when tech-school let out. We only had classes during the week. There was this one fellow from New York, who didn't smoke with any of us airmen. He called us "Poot-butts." The fellows told me don't pay any attention to him because he was on that hard stuff. "What hard stuff," I asked. They said he was on that "Skag". You don't want any of that. I could never understand how he had made it through basic training with a heroin habit, yet instead, how he had been able to enlist as a junkie.

When I went back home on furlough, not only was I an alcoholic, now I was also a pothead. After Tech School, when I arrived at my permanent duty station,

I came to find out what real military life was all about. Most of the enlisted men were alcoholics, and the remainder of them were whoremongers, and or drug addicts. At my duty station I would be intoxicated every week; high on weed; smoking hash; passing out drunk; going AWOL to New York, and to Florida. I was just an alcoholic in a uniform, and every weekend I would be passed out unconscious drunk on my barracks floor. I would be downtown at the various clubs, and pass out drunk. I could vaguely remember being poured into taxi cabs and being driven back to the base. I never knew exactly how I got back to the base and into my barracks. The following mornings I would wake up on the barracks floor, and wonder how I got to where I was. My friends would tell me later about how they had to carry me up the stairs to my dorm. I may have been a drunk, and a pothead, but I was still not inclined to try any Heroin, that came later.

After the military, I rotated back home to the same type of environment that I had been trying to escape from. There is an old saying that we have to watch out for the people, places, and things that will eventually trap you, and that is what I didn't do. One day, one of my very best and oldest friends came down from upstate New York. I hadn't seen him in for many years. We didn't know what he had been up to, but we were soon to find out.

He had a young girl with him who was supposed to be this professional thief, and had a penchant for tricking older men out of their hard-earned money. He was driving this big Lincoln Continental with stagecoach doors, and that isn't all that he had.

There was me, his brother-in-law, and another of our childhood friends when he asked the question, "Do you all get high"? We all said, "Yeah, we got some fire weed." He said, "I am not talking about that baby shit, I'm talking about that real grown man shit." I informed him that I wasn't sticking no needle in my veins, and he said that we didn't have to stick no needle in our veins; all we had to do was skin-pop it. Skin-popping is when you only stick the needle into a big muscle. He said, "Yall won't feel a thing." I was the last one to try it, and to this day, that is the single worst decision that I have ever made.

The feeling of Euphoria that overtook me was indescribable. I had never known such bliss. I said to myself "I'm going to always do this." Little did I know that that was the worst mistake a person could ever make? I have heard people discuss the different types of drugs that people ingest for pleasure purposes, but shooting Heroin is the single most deadly drug affliction imaginable. My friend had a large supply of Heroin, and in the beginning, he was skin-popping us for free, but that soon changed. Afterwards, he informed us that Heroin went for a "dime" a bag, which is ten dollars. After you skin-pop a few times the effects are not as great as before. Therefore, you are forced to start mainlining the Heroin, which is a much more intense high and a lot more deadly. With repeated use, it takes much more of the drug to accomplish the original feeling of the very first high, thus, it begins to cost more. Where you could get high off one bag, now you needed two bags. Instead of requiring ten dollars, now you needed twenty dollars to get high. If you are getting high in the morning, that's twenty dollars; if you are getting high in the afternoon, that's twenty dollars; if you are getting high in the evening, that's twenty dollars; if you are getting high at night, that's twenty dollars; if you are still getting high before going to bed, that's twenty dollars. You can see where this is leading too. Pretty soon you will need a money machine to be able to afford this deadly merry-go-round.

If the drug is highly potent, you will catch a habit on or about the third day. That is when your body starts to react to the absence of the drug in your body. Your own body will start to rebel against you, and demand that you go out and supply it with some more of this intoxicating venom. You most certainly will comply because if you don't, you are in for the most excruciating, and painful experiences of a lifetime. You will definitely find your body some more of that drug, and that's a promise.

You now arrive at the twenty-four thousand dollar question; how do you go out and make from 100 to 200 dollars every day without a job, or any visible means of support, to keep that monkey off of your back? What job pays that sort of money legally, with just a basic high-school education? And the answer is none. Now mind you there are seven days in a week, and Heroin doesn't take the weekends off. So here I am 22years of age, with a nice enough car, an apartment to pay rent for, car notes, insurance, a girlfriend, and a 1400 dollar a week Heroin habit. Am I not already in hell? The amount of criminal activities that I, and those same three individuals that I started doing Heroin with, indulged in is enough crimes to fill up vast pages of many documents. But what is most surprising is that we never physically harmed anybody, although we took everything that wasn't tied down, literally.

I suppose we committed enough crimes to fill up many journals. It would take a lifetime of amends to make up for the crimes that have been committed while trying to maintain a Heroin habit. Now multiply that by about 6 million junkies in the United States alone, and attempt to envision the amount of missing wealth that Heroin took from law-abiding citizens, and you will see why the Federal Government had to take a stand against the Heroin industry. The Heroin epidemic was the single most systemic plague ever to hit this country. You can go on and on about the Crack Cocaine plaque, but Like James Brown said, "Heroin is King."

We would start out shooting Heroin in Florida, but as the seasons changed, we would follow the migrant workers from state to state, looking for a chance to manipulate them out of their money, by hook or by crook.

We would travel to Pennsylvania, and New York in the summer months until the heavy snows hit. Then we would turn around and come right back to Florida. We had to stay close to a Heroin supply or else we would become sick, and that was a fate worth than death. We most often stayed within proximity to New

York City, because that was where the best Heroin always was.

You had to be sharp to cop in New York because some dope fiends there always had their eyes open to con a dummy out of his money if he was not wise. Dope fiends on the East Coast had a trail that they always traveled, lest they find themselves without a place that they could score their product. You could score in Tampa, St. Petersburg, Lakeland, maybe Orlando, Jacksonville, and maybe in Savannah, Ga. After that, you were lucky if you could find some Heroin in Charleston, S.C.

The only place next to cop from was Fayetteville, North Carolina, the home of Ft Braggs Military Base. Military bases had a propensity for having all kind of drugs, during all sorts of times, and Ft. Braggs, North Carolina was no exception.

Everybody was a little leery of Washington, D.C., because it was one of the most dangerous cities on the East Coast. It was notorious for murderers, especially for dopers straggling through there trying to cop dope; so was Philadelphia, Pa. If you stopped in either of those cities and didn't personally know someone, your life wasn't worth a plug nickel.

Now in New York, it was so much dope there that you could throw out a line and dope would show up from everywhere. New York was a dope fiend's dream; it was also his nightmare if you lived there. Fortunately for us, we made our money other places and only went to the city to cop.

Once when we were residing in Allentown, Pa., and went to The City (New York) to cop, and went up into this brownstone building to meet the dealer. There were six dope-fiends lying across this one bed waiting for someone to come in, either to rob or to get them high. We were expensively dressed and had to do some quick thinking. We might have already had a New York Quarter of dope, so we immediately threw it on the table, and said, "Who wants to get high?" Everybody in there reached for their works (syringes), and we hit the door running. We were on the 5th floor; we didn't run down the stairs, we jumped from landing to landing. When we got outside, we were running so fast that our coats were trailing in the breeze. We barely escaped that place with our lives. We never pulled that stunt again. We had plenty of money on us. Quick thinking got us out of a sure robbery, and possibly a double murder. Living life in such a manner as that is not a ticket to a long life.

Committing criminal activity is a surefire way to incur the wrath of the police as well as the establishment, and of course, the odds will catch up with you as they did to us. After being incarcerated, I was sent to a Federal drug treatment center in Dallas Texas for evaluation, to see what level of addiction that I had. It was determined that I was a certified Federal Heroin addict, and I was sent to Lexington, Kentucky's drug treatment Center for a period of time. Sadly to say, there was morphine there also. The compound was flooded with drugs. Instead, of people kicking their addictions, we were still getting high. I think that this was an experimental form of incarceration, because women and men were both there, and we wore our own clothing. If you didn't know better, you would think that you were on the streets of New York, sharpening up your game.

Of course, this was a surefire way for the authorities to study dope fiend behavior, so as to get an assessment of how drug behavior affect different communities. There were heroin addicts there from all over America. The Federal Government eventually shut the place down because of the ongoing drug activity, and because quite a few of the female subjects turned up pregnant. How do you think the taxpayers would have felt had they known that the government was running a program for dope fiends to get high and have fun on the public dime?

When I returned to the streets, I was kind of calm, and had no desire to indulge in drug activity, but eventually, that old itch came back. It didn't come back right away, but it was a gradual awakening. I was living in Bradenton, Florida and was gambling to make a living, and with the tricks that I had learned over the years, I was doing pretty well. My problems started again when I won a sum of money and bought a nice Lincoln Continental. I went to Polk County on a whim and ran into one of my old drugging buddies. He saw me and the car, and suggested that we needed to go to Allentown, Pa. to see these two beautiful ladies that he had left there, and besides, "they will love this car," he said.

He was no longer doing heroin; he was on "Bathtub Crank", a powerful form of methamphetamine that I knew absolutely nothing about. The mention of the beautiful girls was all the incentive that I needed, and I was off to the races again. Wouldn't you know it, one of the girls was a crank addict, and one of the girls was a heroin addict. These relationships would last many years before we would lose contact with the girls again. I indulged in "Meth", but I always ended up back in New York City copping my drug of choice, "heroin". My friend and I eventually fell out because he was the only crank head, and his girl loved heroin. He almost killed her, and I stopped him from killing her, and she fell for me. It wasn't just me; it was also the dope. We had the heroin addiction in common. Of course, she was a "girl of the night", and she was absolutely stunning. She was the type of girl that could stop traffic. Cars would literally stop when they saw her walking down the street. Our relationship couldn't last long because there was never enough dope to satisfy both of our habits, and something would always have to give.

The winter was starting to settle in, and like the birds, us Florida boys always fly south for the winter. If you look up for me when the snow flies, probably, I'll be gone. I would return back and forth over the years, but eventually aids caught up with her and she passed away. It was my good fortune that she contracted the disease after I had had my fling with her. All in all, she was a beautiful person; she just had an addiction that was beyond her control.

Back I Florida, the Crack Cocaine phase was starting up, and I for one didn't see what all the fuss was about. The only cocaine I wanted was some to put in my heroin for a "speedball".

A speedball is when you mix heroin and cocaine together for the purpose of shooting them at the same time. It gives you a rush, and a down feeling at the same time. Later on, dopers would use crack and heroin for the same purpose.

After a while, a person becomes tired of himself, but it was impossible not to shoot heroin when you are addicted to it. Addicted means being a slave to a drug without being able not to indulge in it. Once heroin is In your body for a period of time there is no way you can get over it unless you kick it "cold turkey"(without any other drug to relieve the detox symptoms), or with Methadone. The only way that I have kicked "Cold Turkey" is when I have gone to jail, and I kicked it twice like that. I almost died one of the times. Withdrawal from a heroin habit will physically kill you if there is no one there to administer fluids and give you electrolytes for the maintenance of the body. It once took me eleven days to kick the habit. I was unable to eat anything at all for ten days. A nurse kept me alive by giving me Gatorade, ice, and any kind of light liquid that I could possibly keep down. While kicking, everything that goes into your stomach will come right back up. The body is searching for some heroin. If you put anything into it besides heroin the body will reject it, and purge it back up. It wants the dope, and nothing else will do.

While I'm on this topic, let me tell you about the time while, in Allentown, I rode with this guy who was a Dilaudid expert. Dilaudid is another form of narcotic that is used to relieve pain. It is just as addictive and just as dangerous as heroin. This is what we substituted heroin with if none was available. This one fellow would fake a condition called gallstones. He would prick his finger and mingle the blood with his urine to make sure that blood was in his urine, a surefire sign of gallstones. Doctors prescribe Dilaudid#4 for the intense pain that occurs from trying to pass the gallstones naturally.

Mexican Mud & Finding God

I was running from the law on all counts. I was wanted in three states, but strangely enough, I didn't have a habit at the time although I was using, but not all of the time. I was hiding when my father found me and asked me if I wanted to go to church with him. I thought that I was an atheist, but the trouble that I was in, I needed all the help that I could get. I was wanted for attempted murder, in one state, parole violation in another, and probation violation in another and the police were on my trail. My girlfriend had kids, so I gave her our car. She was afraid to live with me because they had labeled me dangerous, and might shoot on sight. I thought that my father's belief was foolish, but what did I have to lose. I belittled their faith in my mind until I met his Spiritual Advisor. She told me exactly what I had been thinking on the way to see her. She said that I had doubted them in my mind on the way over and that I didn't think that they knew what they were talking about. Anyway, I did as she asked, and got on my knees and began to pray. When I rose up off of my knees, I was a changed man. Not only did I quit doing all drugs, but I also quit lying, cursing, stealing, cheating, and sinning of any kind. Almost immediately my charges got dropped, and the fellow that I had had the gunfight with dropped the attempted murder charges against me because his mother was a member of my newfound church. She told him of the power of God, and the marvelous transformation that had overcome me. My former nemesis hugged me; we both apologized and became friends. Although my being saved and sold out for the Lord didn't last but for about two years, I cannot doubt that something miraculous happened. The only fallout that I had was with my ex-girlfriend. After my charges had been dropped, she came back to me, but since she was a married woman, I couldn't keep company with her because there is no adultery, or as the church folk say," Ain't no sweethearting in God's house."

To show you that there is a power beyond our wildest beliefs, I got this job selling copier systems for this company, and they bought me a nice van, and I became a traveling salesman. Will wonders never cease?

Because I would not see her anymore, my ex-girlfriend and I had a bad argument, and she knocked out the windows of my van, and whatever little bit of religion that I still had also disappeared, because I returned the favor, and knocked out her windows also. The first thing she screamed at me was, "See there! You ain't saved! We could have still been living together". All I know for sure is that a power greater than me tossed all of my troubles into the sea of forgetfulness, and they went away forever. Neither she nor I could have done anything about those problems that is why I had given her the car in the first place so that at least she could look after her family, but she wasn't thankful for that. Although she did love me and didn't want me to go to jail, she still wanted to have everything go her way. Sometimes for better or for worse, we just have to move on. But for that brief interlude, I just have this one thing to say, "Thank God for my father, and thank God for his blessings."

To escape trouble, I left town and went right back into the drug jungle. I felt like I had worn out my welcome on the East coast. I did like I had heard the early settlers do, "Go west young man," although I wasn't so young anymore. If I thought the new synthetic drug that had taken New York by storm in the early eighties was potent (China White), I hadn't reckoned with meeting up with Mr. "Mexican-Mud." I had never before seen Heroin that was not either white or tan until I had started doing "tar." "Black Tar" was the Mexican Mafia's version of heroin. They deliberately leave out a process of the refinement to leave it in a gummy state of existence and package it in balloons. This product is then given the name of "Mexican Mud". It is thought that if you shoot this concoction three times you are hooked. I was already hooked anyway, so it wasn't any skin of off my back, but it was most definitely powerful. It's an amazing thing to realize that you can leave the famous Wilshire Boulevard of Hollywood movie fame and go a few blocks, and be in the midst of a city made or cardboard boxes, and Mexican gangsters with 20 to 30 thousand dollars' worth of narcotics, and money in the center of this cardboard city, and nobody dare mess with them. The police and the city maintenance workers would sometimes come by and push this cardboard mecca down, and within hours, it would be right back up and running, and back in business again.

I don't know what drug demon was driving me, but it seems to me that I was trying to accomplish the feat of having been a coast to coast heroin addict, because I left L.A. and went on to Las Vegas, and then on to

Seattle, Washington. I can't say who controlled the drugs on the west coast, because there are many elements, just as there are many, many forms of illicit drugs out west, but for hard-core heroin addiction, the Mexicans on the west coast rule the roost. That is because many people of Mexican descent also use heroin. My story is not meant to be a research document or a scientific paper, but I do believe that there is an element of truth in the belief that heroin is an alkaloid that attaches itself to the receptor sights in the brains of people of color, more so than others. I know that when I was living in Bethlehem, PA., all the drug addicts in our click were either of black and or Hispanic descent. Seattle, WA. was loaded with Black tar heroin, and there were many junkies of all nationalities living there. Shooting dope in Seattle was no different than shooting dope on the east coast, only that it was much stronger, and more accessible in the Seattle area. I have to admit that there is a darker element in the Seattle area, probably because of the Grunge element, and also because of the Gothic elements.

I had now circumnavigated the country shooting heroin, and was now tired of the race for more and more dope. I only wanted to go home, but King Heroin has the last say in all affairs of addiction.

I eventually made it back home, but still could not shake the habit. It was going on into the millennium (2000), and I happened to get arrested in this small, southern county in Florida. I knew that I was in for a serious time, not because of the charges, but because I had a dual addiction. I was addicted to heroin, and also to #4 Dilaudid, the most powerful form of the Dilaudid that there are. I informed the jail staff that there was going to be a mighty struggle for me to stay alive and that they should put me in the infirmary to better monitor my actions, and to keep me away from the main population because it was going to get ugly. For some reason, they believed me. On day two, I threw up for hours and hours. The trays of food that they were ordered to bring the prisoners started to line up at my cell door. They became afraid because they had never seen inmates not eat. After the sixth day when I had still not eaten anything, they were frantic. The nurse started giving me applesauce, but even that would not stay down. Meanwhile, my body was screaming for me to give it some heroin, or it would kill me. You can actually feel your own body searching itself for any sign of the drug. It craves for the heroin that much. There is no rest for you, you are vomiting, your stomach is balled into a knot, and yet your body is still searching. You drink a little cold water, and immediately your body rejects it, and you throw it back up. Your body only wants the drug, and no substitute will do. You are on the bed one minute, lying on the floor the next minute. You are kneeling in front of the commode heaving yellow bile one minute and delirious the next minute. Around about the ninth or tenth day, your body finally starts to quiet down. The drug has finally left your body. The searching has ceased, and you can, at last, get a little rest, and you feel the first tugging of an appetite. You still can't eat any solid foods, but you can keep a little applesauce down, and are grateful for it. You promise yourself, before God that you will never go through that ordeal again.

You thank the nurse for doing all that she has done to keep you alive. You thank the kitchen staff for trying to give you something that you could keep down. You think the nurse and the kitchen staff for the Gatorade, and for the ice and cold water that they kept supplying you with day and night to keep electrolytes in your body, without which you would have died. It has been a team effort, and you finally realize the ordeal that you have undergone has reached its conclusion. The nurse said to me that she had never seen anything like that in all of her days as a nurse, and if this is what people who abuse heroin go through, then they must all be insane. I totally agreed with her.

After I got my strength back and got my appetite back, I still had to do county time. I went to work in the kitchen and did all that I could do to see that the kitchen ran successfully all the while that I was there. After all, I owed them a debt of gratitude that I could never repay. They had given me my life back, and for that, I was extremely grateful.

After my release, my desire for heroin had taken a hit. Gradually, I started to move in a different circle. The lure of those folks who desire heroin was no longer a part of my psyche; the "pull" was loosening. I went in another direction, and since many of them were dying off, eventually the desire was finally, and miraculously gone. The shackles had finally fallen off my feet. There is an old saying that I remember my mother used to always say to people, but I had never paid it much attention before, and it states, "It's an ill wind that doesn't ever change." Thank God for that wind finally changing.

Recovery Years

After so many years of deviant behavior in order to maintain a Heroin addiction, I almost didn't know just what to do with myself with my newfound freedom. I realized that I had to make a legitimate living, and I was thankful for all of the experiences that I had had over the years in the culinary art career field. I was at least prepared to find employment, because if there was one thing that I had at least learned to do in all of my escapades, it was to cook. Of course, I had to fudge a little bit on my job applications because there were myriad gaps in my employment history.

The first job that I found after my sobriety was dangerous work. I got a job as a water blaster in an industrial cleaning complex. I believe that that job was good therapy. The hourly rates that the job paid was not all that great, but the per diem and the hours on and off the clock were insane. I would work for two hours and then rest for four hours. In the course of the job, we would sometimes accumulate over 100 hours a week. We never worked those hours; they would just award us those hours because we were working 7 days a week. Some schools of thought suggest that you can't work your way out of addiction, but who has a rule on recovery that is set in stone? I didn't have time to think about getting high; I was too busy working. I had informed my baby son's mother that I was now straight, and would try to make amends for all of the suffering that I had caused them with my addiction. She agreed to give us a chance, and we all relocated to Jacksonville, Fla. I worked from sun-up until sun-down. I was making extraordinary money, but money is not always everything. We were spending very little time together. I was proud to be this chief breadwinner, but being a lifelong heroin addict had not prepared me for the normalcy of everyday life. At first, everything was cool. I had started the job in February, and it was now Thanksgiving, and I still had not had a day off. My wife asked me if I was crazy. She asked me who in their right mind worked every day forever. I asked her to give me a little more time so that we could pay the debts that had accumulated through all of my insanity. When I informed her that we were working Christmas day that was the straw which broke the camel's back. She told me that I had traded in one form of insanity for another form of insanity, and if I didn't change, she was taking the kid and going back to her mother's house.

I quit that job, and got a job cooking, and have been cooking ever since. Although we broke up much later because of her drinking, we have remained friends over the years. After all, we have an excellent lad in our son. As a matter of fact, we were both living in the same town when I became sick and was unable to continue working in my chosen field. Little did I realize that way back in Seattle, when I got a job prep-cooking at the Seattle Convention Center that that experience would serve me one day. Although I lied to get the job, I'd never cooked a thing in my life until then. As a matter of fact, my ex is the one that told me to tell that lie. Anyway, it worked out for the good in the end.

I developed a condition in my hands that is caused by a Potassium imbalance in my body that causes my hands and knees, and feet to lock up to the point that I am almost immobilized by that condition. I used to be cooking, and my hands would lock up, and the utensils that I would be using would have to be pried out of my hands. I couldn't fill many orders in that condition, so my days cooking had come to an end. I also developed a disorder called Spasmodic Torticollis which causes a twisting of the neck, almost like Parkinson's disease, but not quite that severe. Needless to say, I needed expert medical attention, and living in Ocala, Florida was not the place to be with these exotic disorders, so I moved to Tampa where the best doctors are located.

I was sitting around trying to stay alive when one day a friend of mine suggested to me that I take a ride with him and his friend. We ended up out here, at Springfield College, Tampa Bay Campus. My friend's friend asked us to come on inside with him because he had to register for college. His hair was as white as snow. I said to him," I have never heard of an old-folks college before." I knew he was too old to be going to college, but Springfield is not like other colleges, and at this school, you are never too old to learn. To make a long story short, He talked me into enrolling, and I now graduate in April 2015 with a Bachelor of Science degree in the Human Services career field.

After all of those maddening years of Heroin addiction, and all of the many escapades, and dangerous adventures, and the many incarcerations, and the near death experiences, how is it possible for me to arrive at this juncture, clothed in my right mind? How is it even possible that I am still alive when so many of my friends have long since departed this life? I know in recovery programs you are not to refer to God, but to your higher power, whomever you chose for that to be. But as for me and my house, this is my summing up my torturous and many faceted ordeals in this life, "There must be a God in Israel, and he has most definitely been watching over me".

Made in the USA
Columbia, SC
18 July 2022